Making
Miniature
Chinese Rugs
& Carpets

Making
Miniature
Chinese Rugs
& Carpets

Carol Phillipson

GUILD OF MASTER CRAFTSMAN PUBLICATIONS

First published 2002 by
Guild of Master Craftsman Publications Ltd,
166 High Street, Lewes,
East Sussex, BN7 1XN

ISBN 1 86108 254 1

Cover and finished photography by Anthony Bailey,
GMC Publications Ltd Photographic Studio
Design and cover design by Phil and Traci Morash at
Fineline Design
Illustrations by John Yates based on original sketches by
Carol Phillipson

Typeface: Optima

Colour origination by Viscan Graphics (Singapore)

Printed and bound by Sun Fung Offset Binding Co Ltd, China

Dedication

This book is dedicated to Ann Hebb for her help in stitching worked samples so beautifully, and for her enthusiasm. Thank you!

Acknowledgements

My grateful thanks go once again to Alan for all his continuing help and support, and to Catherine for her help with stitching.

I am grateful to Spink and Sons of London for permission to adapt designs from their publications.

Again, my sincere thanks go to Sally Jefferson and Coats Patons Crafts UK (01325 394237) for supplying the stranded cottons and silk threads, to Fabric Flair Ltd (0800 716851) for supplying the canvas, and to Appletons Wools (0208 9940711) for the crewel wool.

Contents

Note about 'Threads Required' Keys

Please note that these keys have been computer-generated and the figures given are the exact amounts of thread used to complete the stitches in the designs. Even the most fastidious needleworker is unlikely to measure their thread to within 0.04cm (¹⁄₁₀in), but the keys may offer useful guidelines.

Please also note that, throughout, the left- and right-hand long edge of each rug and carpet is worked with double the thread of the rest of the design, for extra rigidity. This is indicated on the colour charts by a coloured slash, and a corresponding slash symbol in the same colour thread in the 'Threads required' key. In addition, a footnote is included in the key with guidance on the number of strands you should work the edges.

Preface

While I was researching my last book, *Chinese Cross Stitch Designs*, I was really pleased to be asked to write a book on Chinese miniature carpets. This gave me the opportunity to extend my research in order to accumulate a selection of designs from many sources, which show a variety of colour, pattern, borders and functions. Completing this proved to be very enjoyable: so pleasurable in fact, that I almost think it should carry a health warning! It can be quite addictive, because while the rugs are quite a challenge, the end results are so varied and lovely.

I have included rugs from mainland China and also from Chinese (Eastern) Turkestan, which is now in the Chinese province of Sinkiang. All of the designs were adapted from carpets from the seventeenth, eighteenth and nineteenth centuries, and are stitched using either stranded cotton, silk or crewel wool.

At the end of the book I have included a full colour thread conversion chart (see page 88) so that you will be able you to stitch every one of the Chinese rugs and carpet projects in any of the threads.

Map of the
Old Silk Route

c. AD 600

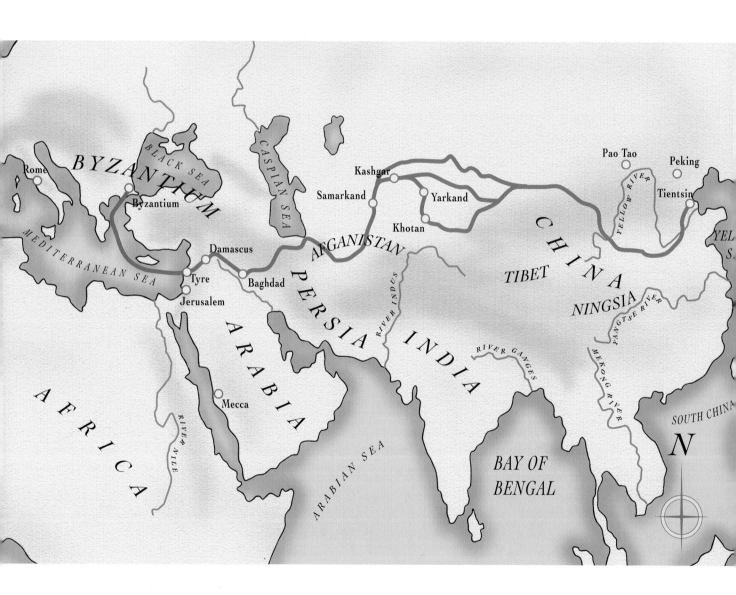

Introduction to Chinese Carpets

While Marco Polo alludes to carpet production in China in the thirteenth century, today's oldest surviving Chinese carpets are from the Ming dynasty (1368–1644).

Carpets were primarily made in the northern provinces of China, the main centres of production being Ningsia, Kansu, Pao Tao, Peking and Tientsin. The intense heat and humidity of the central and southern regions made the carpets deteriorate, which meant that straw mats were more appropriate in these parts of the country. Misleadingly, carpets were routinely named after places from which they were marketed and exported, rather than where they were originally made: Samarkand, Kashgars or Khotan, for example.

The Old Silk Route

The Silk Route – or Silk Road – is the ancient caravan route linking China and the West, along which silk was carried westwards and wool, gold and silver transported eastwards.

Originating in Siam, it was 4,000 miles (6,400 kilometres) long and followed the Great Wall of China to the northwest and, bypassing the deserts, it climbed mountains to cross Afghanistan and eventually reached the Levant. From here merchandise was shipped across the Mediterranean Sea. The Silk Route was treacherous and, because of its various dangers, fell into disuse, but the Mongols revived it in the thirteenth century.

Early Chinese traders would sell their silk to the Parthians and they then sold it on to the Romans at the exchange rate of one ounce of gold for one ounce of silk.

Form and function

Carpets were made from the wool of sheep, goats and camels, and at times from waste silk. The silk came from damaged cocoons which prevented it from being reeled off to make silk thread. Instead, it had to be 'carded' (combed and cleaned prior to spinning) in the same way as wool to make it suitable for producing carpets. A few rugs and carpets were made from velvet and felt, and some also had metallic gold or silver threads woven into the background. For my own miniature versions, I have used stranded cotton, wool and 100% silk thread.

Carpets were hand-woven on looms and knotted with Persian or Ghiordes knots. An average-sized carpet contained over a million knots; a skilled weaver might work several thousand knots each day. I have used the Ghiordes knot to create the fringes on my miniature carpets. Fringing was a way of fastening off the warp threads to secure the

Saddle rug from China (textile) (The Nicholas M. Salgo Collection, USA/Bridgeman Art Library)

ends neatly, and these were therefore the same colour as the warp thread. However, I have sometimes taken the liberty of altering the colour for my designs.

Chinese carpets differed from other oriental carpets because the designs made use of symbolism, rather than being purely decorative. The centre – or field – of the carpets was mainly a plain background with designs set on it, often with wonderful borders. The colour combinations were quite limited; sometimes as few as two were used. Blue, in a variety of shades, is nearly always present.

Carpets were made to perform several functions. In the north, rugs were mainly used for covering the 'stove bed'. A stove bed was a pile of bricks covered with a rug which, during the day, was used as a comfortable seat and warmed along with the rest of the house. At night, it was transformed into a bed.

Pillar rugs

Unique to China, pillar rugs were always made in pairs. They were long and narrow and specially designed to be skilfully wrapped around the long cylindrical pillars in temples and palaces, rather than to cover beds and floors. Laid flat, the pattern appears disjointed, but when fastened around the pillars, the dragon spirals around and the borders join up to complete the design. Nearly all pillar rugs have a tasselled border at the top and the Holy Mountain rising from water and waves at the bottom.

As pillar rugs were made of wool, I have stitched the miniature versions of these that appear in this book in crewel wool.

Saddle rugs

Saddle rugs were not, as one might imagine, simply for sitting on, but were mounted under the saddletree – the frame of the saddle – to form a padded protective barrier at either side of the horse's body against the effects of dust, dirt and moisture.

To function efficiently, they needed to be made very strong, and were lined with a blue cotton fabric. Chinese saddle rugs were made in two identical halves which were then stitched securely together.

Prayer rugs

Prayer rugs or 'saphs' were other specialist rugs, although not exclusive to China. They were used by devout Moslems for either kneeling or standing on during their daily prayers. Each mosque has a 'Mihrab' (prayer niche) in its walls pointing to Mecca and, in preparation for saying his prayers, a Moslem man points his prayer rug in this direction.

The design of a prayer rug usually incorporates a mihrab. Mihrabs are often placed side by side to make a 'saph', a larger rug, to enable the whole family to pray at once. Five mihrabs is a usual number, but some saphs may have as many as ten or eleven. Multi-niche prayer rugs with five or more mihrabs in a row were a speciality of the Khotans from East Turkestan.

Dyeing carpets

Older carpets were dyed with natural dyes which offered a restricted palette. Available to the carpet maker were blues from indigo (a plant native to China), yellows from saffron and turmeric, reds from the roots of the climbing plant madder or from cochineal which was imported, and a few shades of green, which came from leaves. Green was a sacred colour, so it was considered improper to use in a carpet which would be trodden on. Shades of brown came from either natural camel's wool, oak bark, pomegranate and vine leaves. Cream was created from natural sheep's wool. The only colour to come from a mineral was black, which was extracted from iron oxide.

Chinese carpet manufacturers did not dye the whole hank of wool at once, but in individual

Dyeing and Winding Silk, from 'China in a Series of Views' by George Newenham Wright (1790–1877) engraved by G. Paterson, 1843 (coloured engraving) by Thomas Allom (1804–72) (after) (Private collection/The Stapleton Collection/Bridgeman Art Library)

long strands. These were then rinsed well in cold water or placed in a running stream, then dried in the open air. As one might imagine, it was impossible to dye two strands to exactly the same shade, producing slight variations in colour in each carpet. Many natural colours faded with age, but indigo kept its colour well.

Aniline dyes were introduced into China in the twentieth century. Because they were synthetic, they offered more recent carpet makers an almost unlimited choice of colour.

Patterns and borders

Although Chinese carpets had a restricted colour range compared with most other oriental carpets, they more than made up for this with their wonderful borders and patterns.

Most of the patterns fell into four main categories: the 'Tree of Life', flowers such as the peony, Gül patterns (octagonal or lozenge shapes) and Taoist or Buddhist auspicious characters and symbols. Very rarely were humans represented, except occasionally a Buddha, but favourite animals were used, including dragons, phoenixes, bats, stags and fo-dogs.

'Tree of Life'

'Tree of Life' designs represent a plant, very often a pomegranate tree, which signifies a wish for fertility and many sons. The motif shows the tree growing out of a vase and spreading its branches over the carpet. The vase is a symbol of water, the trunk of the tree represents the father and the branches are the children. This design is often found on prayer rugs.

Peonies

Peonies are known as the Flowers of Plenty and are a symbol of wealth and prosperity. They are often woven into rug designs as central medallions with creeping foliage. Peonies also signify spring.

Gül patterns

Gül patterns are usually octagonal or lozenge shapes repeated over the rug to form a pattern.

Auspicious symbols

Auspicious symbols are found throughout China and occur in all art forms, including carpet design. They carry a symbolic message normally relating to a wish for good fortune, fertility, wisdom or long life. Some of the signs are directly connected with the characteristics of the object: for example, pear trees live for many years and therefore represent longevity. Pines also signify a wish for a long life and an easy death. A lotus stands for purity because it grows in muddy water, but emerges white and unblemished. It also represents Buddha who survived this corrupt world pure and holy.

Homophones

Homophones give meaning to some characters. For instance, the word for butterfly is 'die' which is phonetically identical to the word meaning seventy or eighty years. A butterfly therefore represents a wish for long life, even though some butterflies live for less than a day.

Other symbolization

Almost all Chinese carpets have a border, either all the way round or at the top and bottom. Many of the early rugs and carpets had variations of scroll or fret patterns and swastikas. The swastika is a symbol for luck and happiness which also means ten thousand or 'wan' and, when combined with other symbols, it multiplies a wish many times over.

Clouds, waves, mountains, earth and fire often form a dramatic border at the ends of a carpet, although clouds are used throughout carpet

design. The symbolization of these motifs is almost graphic: waves are represented by parallel wavy bands, calm water as curves and spray as dots. Mountains are shown rising up from the water, with the Holy Mountain being the highest in the centre. Fire is often depicted in conjunction with a dragon, flames flickering around the 'pearl'.

Traditionally, all Chinese lakes and rivers are supposed to be guarded by dragons who live in underwater crystal palaces surrounded by priceless treasures. They eat opals and pearls, which is why dragons are frequently illustrated holding or chasing flaming pearls. The pearl is a symbol for purity, which the dragon spends its whole life trying to attain. Dragons symbolize the emperor of China.

As you work through the designs in this book, I explain in more detail specific aspects of the ways in which Chinese symbols are used to give a basic understanding of their importance in Chinese rug and carpet making.

Chinese rug with golden border of flowerheads and scrolling motifs surrounding a terracotta field depicting two dragons (Private collection/Bonhams/ Bridgeman Art Library)

Equipment and Materials

There are just a few basic pieces of equipment and materials required to enable you to attempt to stitch any (or all) of the designs in this book.

A selection of tools and materials for making miniature Chinese rugs and carpets, including: needles, two pairs of scissors, stranded cotton threads, crewel wool threads, 22-count fabric and a magnet board (optional)

Equipment

Scissors

Scissors are important. I have two pairs of needlework scissors: the first is a small, sharp, pointed pair which I use for threads. I have even fastened a piece of wool on the handle to remind the rest of the family. I also have a large pair for

cutting canvas. I use another pair of scissors altogether to cut paper, as this notoriously blunts even the sharpest scissors.

Magnets
The most invaluable item I have recently acquired, is a small pair of round magnets which fit on either side of the fabric that is being stitched and trap the chart, so that it is always conveniently in view at the edge of the embroidery frame. They also keep needles safe when not in use.

Light
A good light is a wise investment. There are many lamps specifically designed for embroiderers, but I find a well-placed spotlight equally acceptable.

Needles
Blunt-ended needles should always be used for counted-thread work because they do not split and weaken the threads. I have used a size 22 or 24 needle for the rugs and carpet designs in this book.

Frames
The type of frames you use is a matter of personal preference. Some stitchers never use one, while others always do. While it is tempting sometimes not to bother, I always use one because I find the end result more pleasing. It certainly minimizes the need for stretching and adjusting the work later.

All my recent canvas work and large projects have been completed using clip frames. They are a recent innovation, and composed of lightweight plastic tubes with clips that can be adapted to a variety of sizes. To use, the fabric is simply laid over the frame and tensioners are placed over the top to keep it in place. A simple twist adjusts the tension. They really have taken the hard work out of mounting fabric onto a frame and, moreover, do not damage or mark the fabric. I used a small clip frame for each of the Chinese rugs and carpets in this book.

Materials

Fabric
All designs were worked on 22-count canvas. The finished size of each stitched rug is given in the instructions. I like to allow an additional 7.5cm (3in) extra fabric all the way round, so I recommend cutting the canvas 15cm (6in) larger than the size given.

Threads
Eighteen of the rugs and carpets were stitched using three strands of Anchor Stranded Cotton, three use a single strand of Appletons Crewel Wool and four are stitched in three strands of Kreinik Silk Mori which is 100% silk.

Where a particular thread is unavailable, please refer to the conversion chart at the end of the book which lists alternative brands of threads in the nearest equivalent colour, though they are probably not identical. Where I do not consider a colour to have a close enough match, I have marked it with a star.

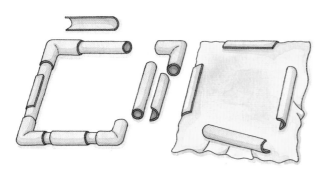

A clip frame

Stitches and Techniques

All rug and carpet designs in this book are worked in tent stitch. This gives a better, denser covering than half-cross stitch, and the thread covers the back of the canvas for a neat finish.

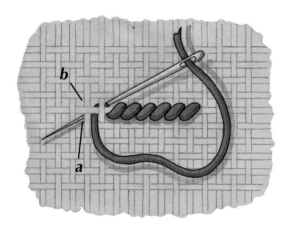

Tent stitch

Finishing the rugs

Once the stitching is complete and the long edge has been worked using double thread, take a look at your work and decide whether your rug or carpet needs stretching back into shape.

Reshaping

To reshape, lightly dampen the work and leave for a minute to soften the canvas. Pin it out onto a board using drawing pins, making sure that the corners are square. Do not strain the canvas too much or it will pull the edges into scallop shapes. Let it dry naturally then remove from the board.

Working the fringe

Next work the fringes at each end of the rug or carpet with Ghiordes knots (see facing opposite). Thread a needle using six strands of stranded cotton, six strands of silk or two strands of wool.

1 With the stitching facing away from you and the right side uppermost, insert the needle downwards into the second hole from the left-hand side (**a**), then bring it back up through the first hole (on the left), so that the thread has gone around one canvas thread. Leave an end about 5cm (2in) long.
2 Take the needle over two threads to the right and around the next thread from right to left (**b**). Repeat this process, but instead of leaving an end as you have at the beginning, leave a loop approximately 4cm (1½in) long.
3 Once the end of the rug is complete, cut the loops and trim to about (2.5cm) 1in to form a fringe. Repeat this method to complete the fringe at the other end.

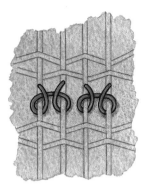

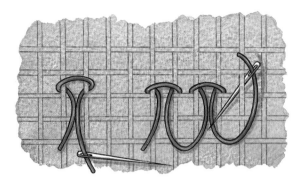

Original Ghiordes knot

Adaptation of Ghiordes knot for rug fringes

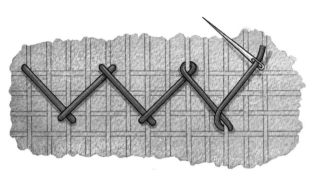

Herringbone stitch

Tidying the work

To tidy the finished work, trim the four sides of the rug to approximately 2cm (¾in) all the way round, then turn it back and either stick the excess onto the underside of the rug or, using herringbone stitch (see left and below), stitch it down with some cotton thread.

Tidy the back of the miniature rugs and carpets with herringbone stitch

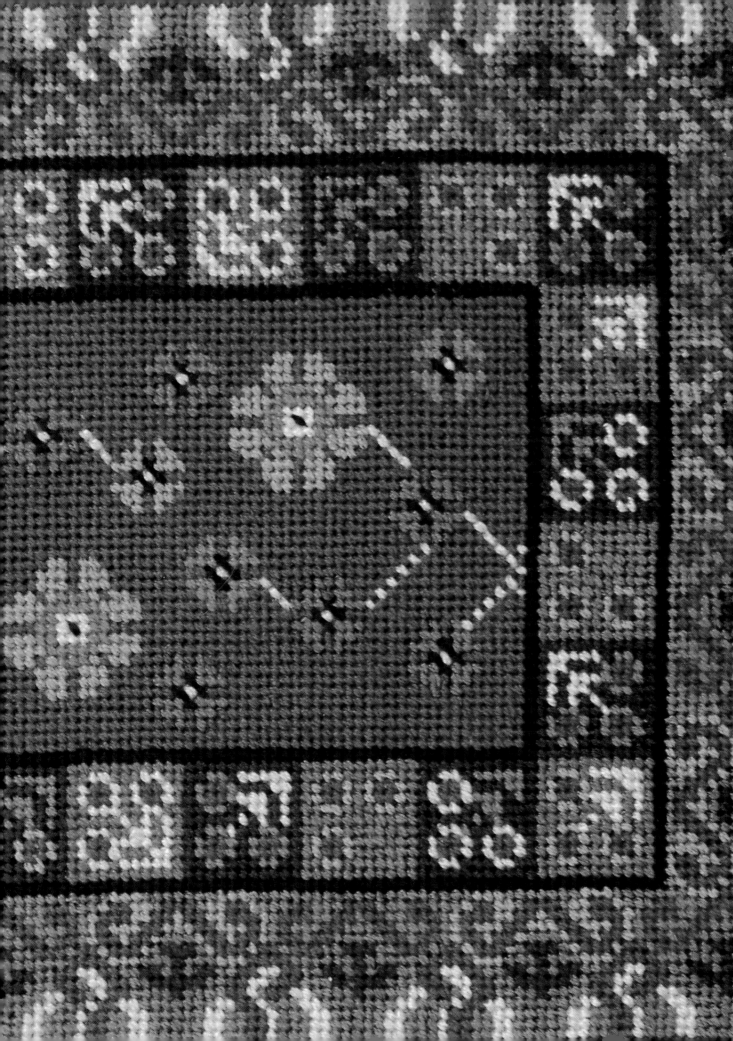

The Designs

East Turkestan 'Tree of Life' Carpet

This nineteenth-century carpet is a perfect example of a 'Tree of Life' with a pomegranate pattern growing from a vase. The colouring is somewhat unusual because similar designs most often have green foliage and red pomegranates. Pomegranates are used in many Chinese art forms to symbolize fertility because of the vast number of seeds contained in the fruit. The flower border used here is typical of Samarkand carpets, but is not as common in older Chinese rugs. It is bordered by a T-border.

Design size	12.8 x 16.7cm (5 x 6⅝in)
Stitch count	111 x 145
Number of strands	3
Number of strands for fringe	6
Thread for fringe	Anchor Stranded Cotton 1014

Threads required

	Anchor Stranded Cotton	Amount
	1014	2281.7cm (898⅜in)
	311	3059.6cm (1204¾in)
	139	207.7cm (81¾in)
	386	830.1cm (326⅝in)
	338	606.9cm (238⅞in)
	1014*	128.2cm (50½in)

*Work at end using 6 strands

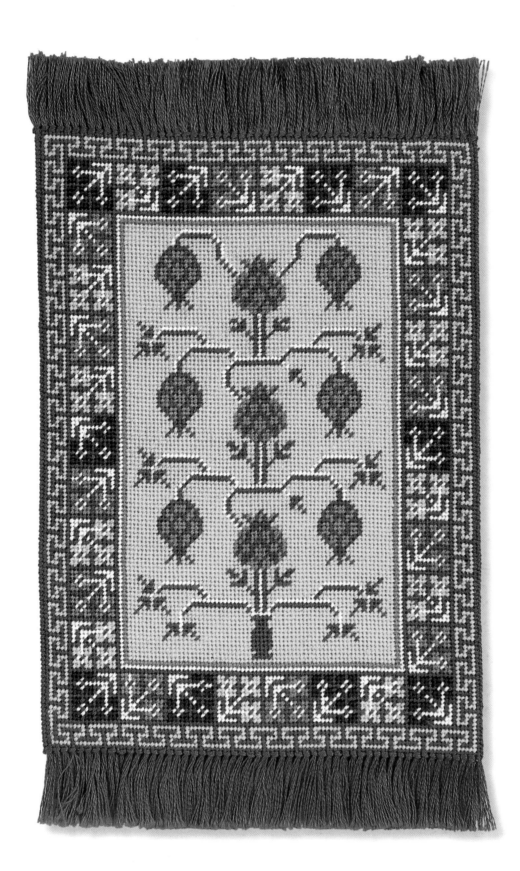

EAST TURKESTAN 'TREE OF LIFE' CARPET

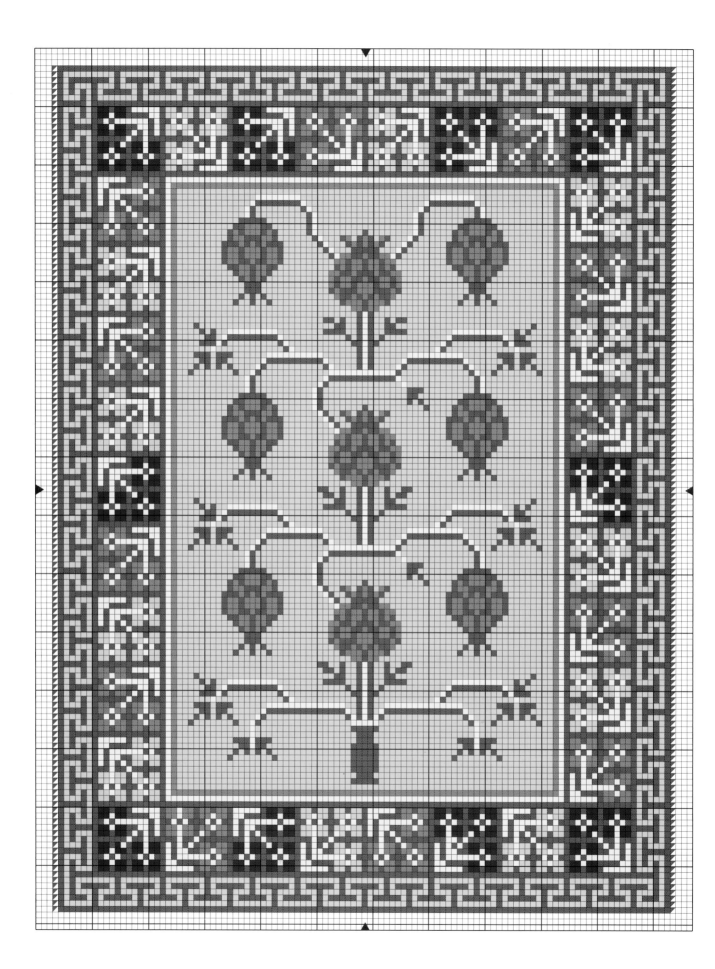

Blue Buddhist Pillar Rug

a

c

T his design was adapted from a nineteenth-century pillar rug. The Buddhist symbols of the original are more freely scattered about the rug. The symbols were taken from the 'Eight Emblems of Good Fortune', a source of auspicious symbols based on religious and traditional beliefs, which were alleged to have been seen in Buddha's footprints. This design shows the conch shell (a) which signifies the calling of the people to worship, a canopy (b) which signifies protection of the people from harm, a wheel (c) which represents the law and, finally, a destiny or everlasting knot (d) for the constant and never-ending mercy of Buddha.

The top of this rug has a lovely border of tassels, typical of pillar rugs, and the border at the bottom shows the Holy Mountain rising up from waves and spray.

b

d

Threads required

	Appletons Crewel Wool	Amount
■	852	7889cm (3105⅜in)
▨	721	771.7cm (303⅞in)
■	823	600.2cm (236⅜in)
▨	693	1458.6cm (574⅜in)
▨	765	355.4cm (139⅞in)
◣	852*	254.6cm (100⅜in)

*2 strands wool

Design size	10.3 x 16.6cm (4 x 6¹⁷⁄₃₂in)
Stitch count	98 x 125
Number of strands	1
Number of strands for fringe	2
Thread for fringe	Appletons Crewel Wool 852

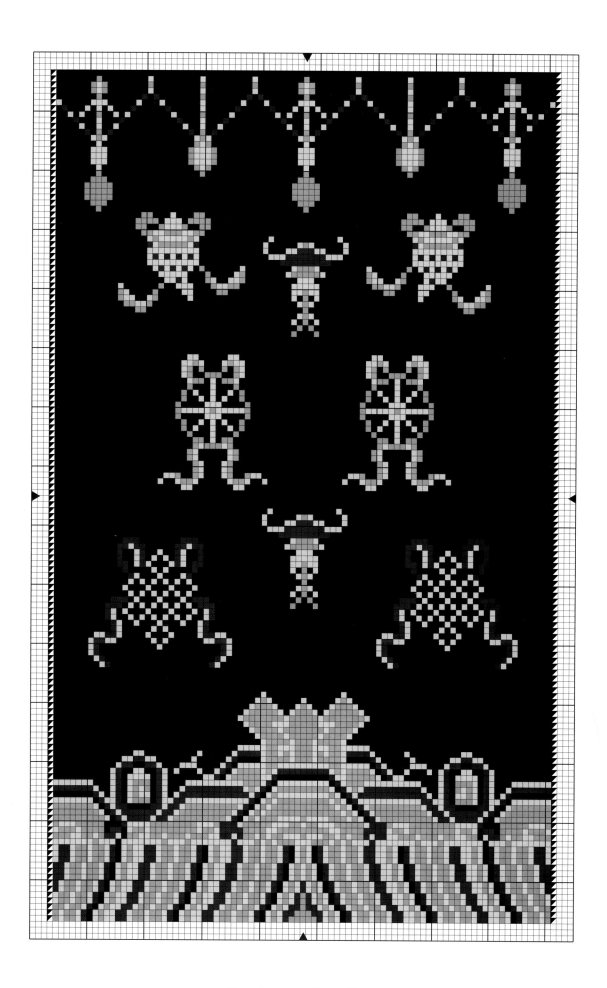

BLUE BUDDHIST PILLAR RUG

17

Nineteenth-century Khotan Carpet

I have put together components from several mid-nineteenth-century Khotan carpets to make this attractive rug. Khotan is in Sinkiang (Chinese Turkestan) which became part of China during the eighteenth century, and is on the original Silk Route. It has the typical Turkestan flower border and around that a further border pattern called Yün Tsai T'ou or 'Cloudhead'. This pattern is similar to a wave, but with horns. At the edges is a border of dots called a 'Pearl' border. The combination of colour was inspired by a saddle rug. This rug was a particularly interesting project to stitch because of the intricate pattern and attractive colouring.

Design size	11.3 x 14.4cm (4⁷⁄₁₆ x 5²⁄₃in)
Stitch count	111 x 145
Number of strands	3
Number of strands for fringe	6
Thread for fringe	Anchor Stranded Cotton 386

Threads required

	Anchor Stranded Cotton	Amount
	386	501.2cm (197³⁄₁₀in)
	843	377.9cm (148⁸⁄₁₀in)
	176	776.2cm (305⁶⁄₁₀in)
	69	1893.1cm (745³⁄₁₀in)
	890	382.8cm (150⁷⁄₁₀in)
	338	600.7cm (236⁵⁄₁₀in)
	150	238.7cm (94in)
	123	533.5cm (210in)
	69*	110.5cm (43⁵⁄₁₀in)

*Work at end using 6 strands

NINETEENTH-CENTURY KHOTAN CARPET

Wool Foliage Dragon Carpet

At first glance, this nineteenth-century carpet appears to be a chaotic mass of foliage and branches, but, in fact, contains fourteen stylized sprawling dragons called foliage dragons. This format is typical, with its matching central medallion and corner motifs and the depiction of geometric or naturalistic dragons. In amongst the dragons are flaming pearls (see page 4).

Design size	12.8 x 18.5cm (5 x 7⁹⁄₃₂in)
Stitch count	111 x 160
Number of strands	1
Number of strands for fringe	2
Thread for fringe	Appletons Crewel Wool 722

Threads required

	Appletons Crewel Wool	Amount
	992	463.2cm (182⁴⁄₁₀in)
	749	4308.7cm (1696³⁄₁₀in)
	824	887.6cm (349⁴⁄₁₀in)
	722	3232cm (1272⁴⁄₁₀in)
	694	730.2cm (287⁵⁄₁₀in)
	724	5795.6cm (2281⁷⁄₁₀in)
	724*	282.9cm (111⁴⁄₁₀in)

*Work at end using 2 strands

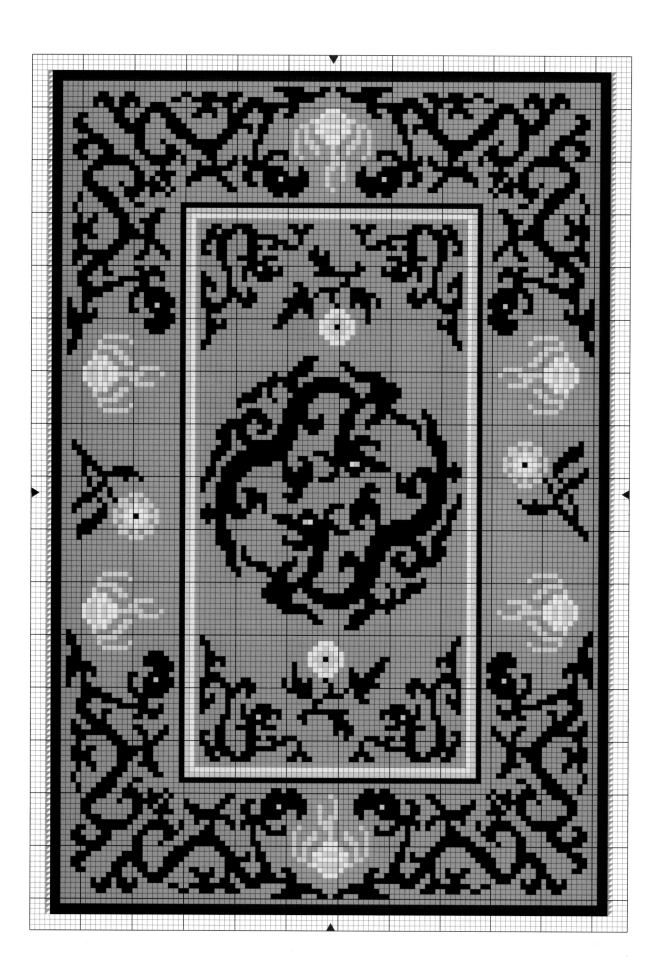

Cream Foliage Dragon Carpet

This design has been adapted from a camel-hair carpet dated circa 1700. It illustrates foliage dragons and is bordered by an impressive vine. The original carpet also had a fret border with swastikas. Legs and tails wrapped around the heads form the medallion in the centre, and there are more foliage dragon motifs in each corner. Again, this rug has a limited range of colours, but the original camel's wool would have given a darker background.

Design size	10.9 x 15.5cm (4⁵⁄₃₂ x 6³⁄₃₂in)
Stitch count	94 x 134
Number of strands	3
Number of strands for fringe	6
Thread for fringe	Anchor Stranded Cotton 275

Threads required

	Anchor Stranded Cotton	Amount
	386	3090.5cm (1216⁷⁄₁₀in)
	150	1815.8cm (714⁹⁄₁₀in)
	215	196.3cm (77³⁄₁₀in)
	214	346.5cm (136⁴⁄₁₀in)
	150*	118.5cm (46⁶⁄₁₀in)

*Work at end using 6 strands

CREAM FOLIAGE DRAGON CARPET

'Shou' Rug

This rug was adapted from an early nineteenth-century narrow runner which was over eleven feet long. It shows two 'Shou' characters, but the original had three motifs with a largely plain background. 'Shou' characters occur in various forms throughout Chinese design and symbolize a wish for longevity. I added a border from a late eighteenth-century carpet.

Design size	9.7 x 14.1cm (3 13/16 x 5 9/16in)
Stitch count	84 x 122
Number of strands	3
Number of strands for fringe	6
Thread for fringe	Anchor Stranded Cotton 368

Threads required

	Anchor Stranded Cotton	Amount
	369	84.9cm (33 4/10in)
	150	1112.1cm (437 8/10in)
	390	286.4cm (112 8/10in)
	147	142.3cm (56in)
	368	1188.1cm (467 8/10in)
	5975	1608cm (633 1/10in)
	150*	107.9cm (42 5/10in)

*Work at end using 6 strands

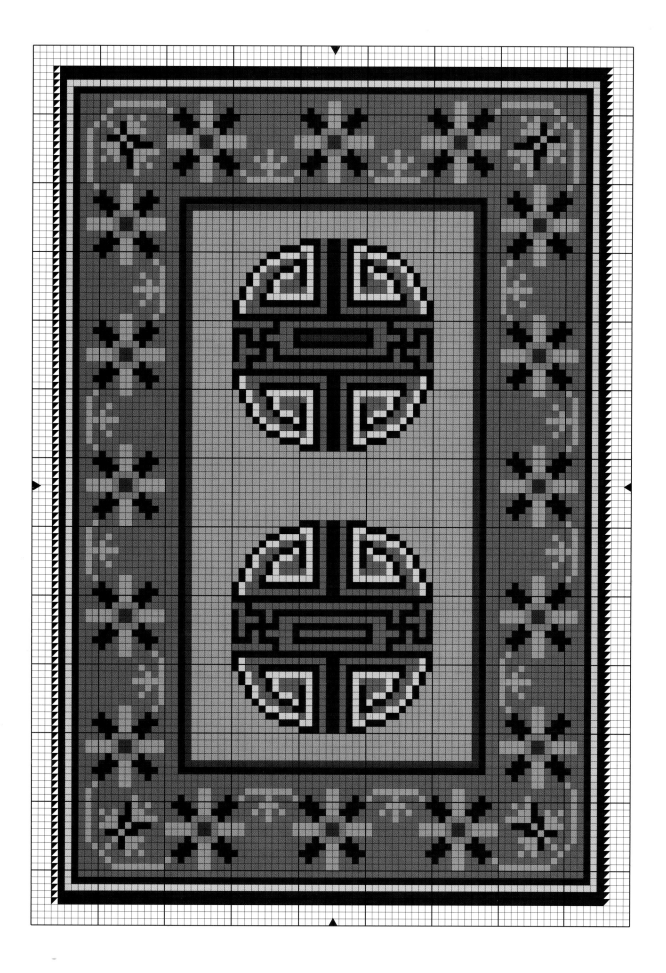

'SHOU' RUG

Silk Dragon Carpet

I used Kreinik Silk Mori for this nineteenth-century rug. It is very pleasant to work with and gives a soft texture to the finished carpet. There are many Chinese carpets with a similar design, but I chose this one because of the attractive combination of colours. The design illustrates dragons chasing a pearl among the clouds. The border depicts waves, calm water and mountains.

Design size	9.6 x 18cm (3¾ x 7³⁄₃₂in)
Stitch count	83 x 156
Number of strands	3
Number of strands for fringe	6
Thread for fringe	Kreinik Silk Mori 7126

Threads required

	Kreinik Silk Mori	Amount
	7128	41.5cm (16⁴⁄₁₀in)
	7126	2626.9cm (1034²⁄₁₀in)
	5016	603.3cm (237⁵⁄₁₀in)
	5095	497.3cm (195⁸⁄₁₀in)
	7124	713cm (280⁷⁄₁₀in)
	7133	191.8cm (75⁵⁄₁₀in)
	7135	138.8cm (54⁶⁄₁₀in)
	7134	312.9cm (123²⁄₁₀in)
	7126*	137.9cm (54³⁄₁₀in)
	7014	459.7cm (181in)

*Work at end using 6 strands

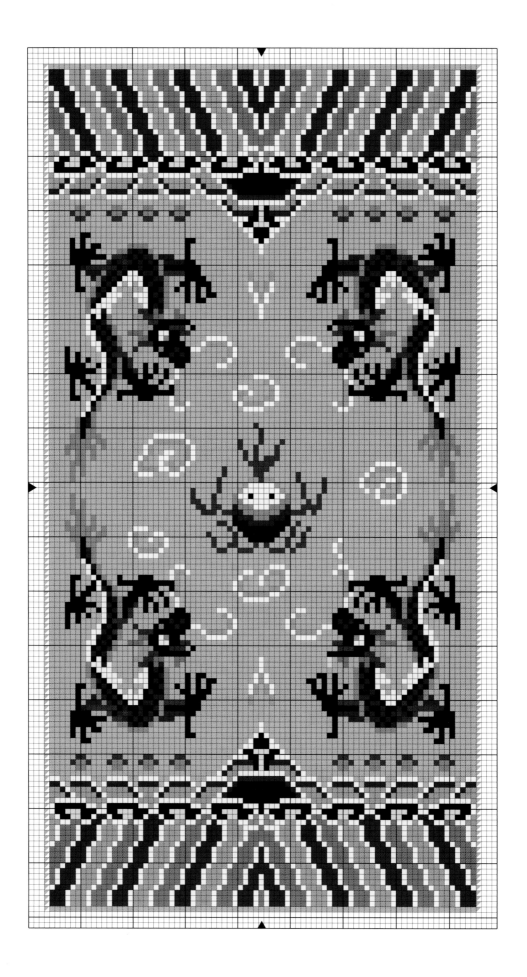

Orange Medallion Carpet

T his is a small rug, with a design adapted from the medallions visible on the overall pattern shown on an eighteenth-century scroll painting. The anonymous painting was a portrait of the Empress Xiaoxian wearing her court robes, and showed the dais on the carpet. I added a border to the medallions based on a pattern shown on the dais.

Design size	8 x 14.4cm (3⅛ x 5⅔in)
Stitch count	69 x 125
Number of strands	3
Number of strands for fringe	6
Thread for fringe	Anchor Stranded Cotton 390

Threads required

	Anchor Stranded Cotton	Amount
	326	387.6cm (152⁹⁄₁₀in)
	311	2370.9cm (933⁴⁄₁₀in)
	341	116.7cm (45⁹⁄₁₀in)
	323	533.1cm (209⁹⁄₁₀in)
	380	293.5cm (115⁵⁄₁₀in)
	380*	110.5cm (43⁵⁄₁₀in)

*Work at end using 6 strands

Dragon Pillar Rug

I have adapted this design from a nineteenth-century pillar rug. The original was actually 105cm x 320cm (3ft 6in x 10ft 5in). It illustrates a dragon among the clouds, chasing the elusive pearl. The dragon, a representation of the emperor, is a symbol of goodwill and protector of the people.

Design size	11.9 x 19.1cm (4¹¹⁄₁₆ x 7½in)
Stitch count	103 x 165
Number of strands	1
Number of strands for fringe	2
Thread for fringe	Appletons Crewel Wool 722

Threads required

	Appletons Crewel Wool	Amount
	722	9127.5cm (3593⁵⁄₁₀in)
	312	823cm (324in)
	749	1287.1cm (506⁷⁄₁₀in)
	992	1411.8cm (555⁵⁄₁₀in)
	744	688.7cm (271¹⁄₁₀in)
	748	1201.4cm (473in)
	855	191.8cm (75⁵⁄₁₀in)
	722*	292.6cm (115²⁄₁₀in)

*Work at end using 2 strands

DRAGON PILLAR RUG

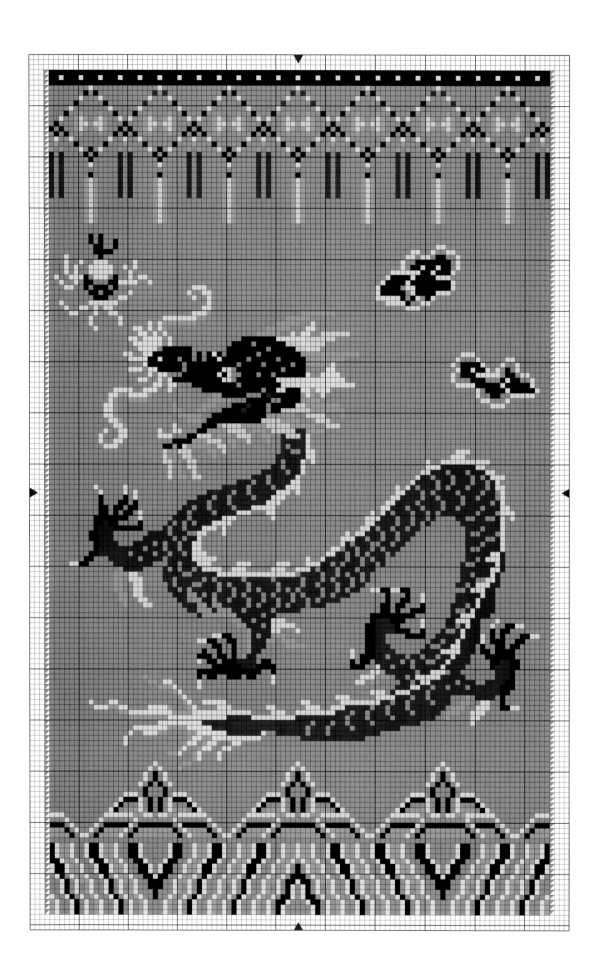

Blue Saddle Rug

This design was adapted from a nineteenth century Kansu saddle rug. It shows destiny knots which signify a wish for a safe journey through life under the protection of Buddha. Kansu rugs tended to be small and were usually restricted to combinations of white and blue. Kansu was on the Old Silk Route to Peking, and indigo grew profusely in this area which accounts for the blue. The white came from undyed sheep's wool. As it was only a small rug, I stitched it in silk, and am pleased with the effect here, but this obviously would have been most unsuitable for a practical item.

Design size	9.7 x 11.4cm (3¹³⁄₁₆ x 4½in)
Stitch count	84 x 100
Number of strands	3
Number of strands for fringe	6
Thread for fringe	Anchor Stranded Cotton 390

Threads required

	Kreinik Silk Mori	Amount
	5016	793cm (312²⁄₁₀in)
	2026	76cm (29⁹⁄₁₀in)
	5057	1402.1cm (552in)
	2024	53cm (20⁹⁄₁₀in)
	7128	1300.4cm (512in)
	5016*	88.4cm (434⁸⁄₁₀in)

*Work at end using 6 strands

Ming Dragon Carpet

This richly coloured seventeenth-century design was inspired by a very worn silk carpet from the Ming dynasty (1368–1644). It is one of the oldest surviving Chinese carpets and the colours are now extremely faded. The design shows a dragon among clouds, and on the original there is a flaming pearl, but because of space limitations, I have chosen to leave this out of the design. The border is once again the Yün Tsai T'ou or Cloudhead. There is a scattering of Taoist symbols, particularly vases and books, on the field of the original.

Design size	9.6 x 14.9cm (3¾ x 5²⁷⁄₃₂in)
Stitch count	83 x 129
Number of strands	3
Number of strands for fringe	6
Thread for fringe	Anchor Stranded Cotton 386

Threads required

	Anchor Stranded Cotton	Amount
	20	2272.4cm (894⁹⁄₁₀in)
	307	322.2cm (126⁹⁄₁₀in)
	152	335.9cm (132³⁄₁₀in)
	268	362.4cm (142⁷⁄₁₀in)
	891	178.6cm (70³⁄₁₀in)
	943	644cm (253⁵⁄₁₀in)
	386	389.9cm (153⁵⁄₁₀in)
	149	113.2cm (44⁵⁄₁₀in)
	20*	114cm (44⁹⁄₁₀in)

*Work at end using 6 strands

MING DRAGON CARPET

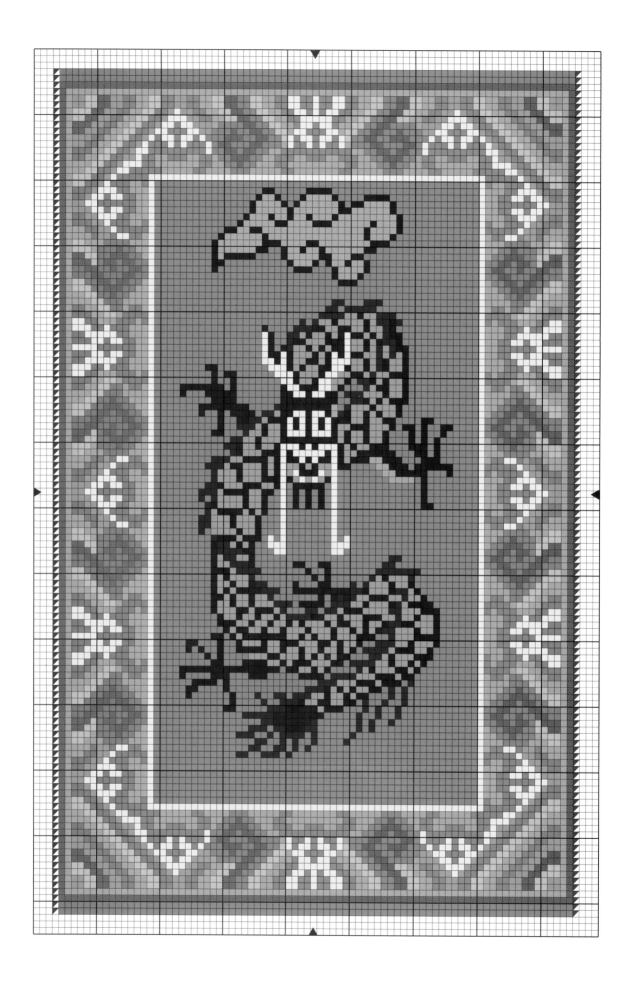

East Turkestan Prayer Rug

L ike the majority of prayer rugs, this one from the eighteenth century shows the 'Tree of Life' design. Executed in silk, this rug has ten mihrabs, each one based on a variation of the 'Tree of Life'. I have made use of just one of them for my miniature version of this rug. Around the edge is a dotted 'Pearl' border.

Design size	8.9 x 13.4cm (3½ x 5⁹/₃₂in)
Stitch count	77 x 116
Number of strands	3
Number of strands for fringe	6
Thread for fringe	Kreinik Silk Mori 7124

Threads required

	Kreinik Silk Mori	Amount
	3015	703.7cm (277in)
	3021	263.4cm (103⁷/₁₀in)
	5097	1277cm (502⁷/₁₀in)
	7124	518.5cm (204¹/₁₀in)
	7126	116.7cm (45⁹/₁₀in)
	7133	282.4cm (111²/₁₀in)
	7135	683.8cm (269²/₁₀in)
	7135*	102.5cm (40⁴/₁₀in)

*Work at end using 6 strands

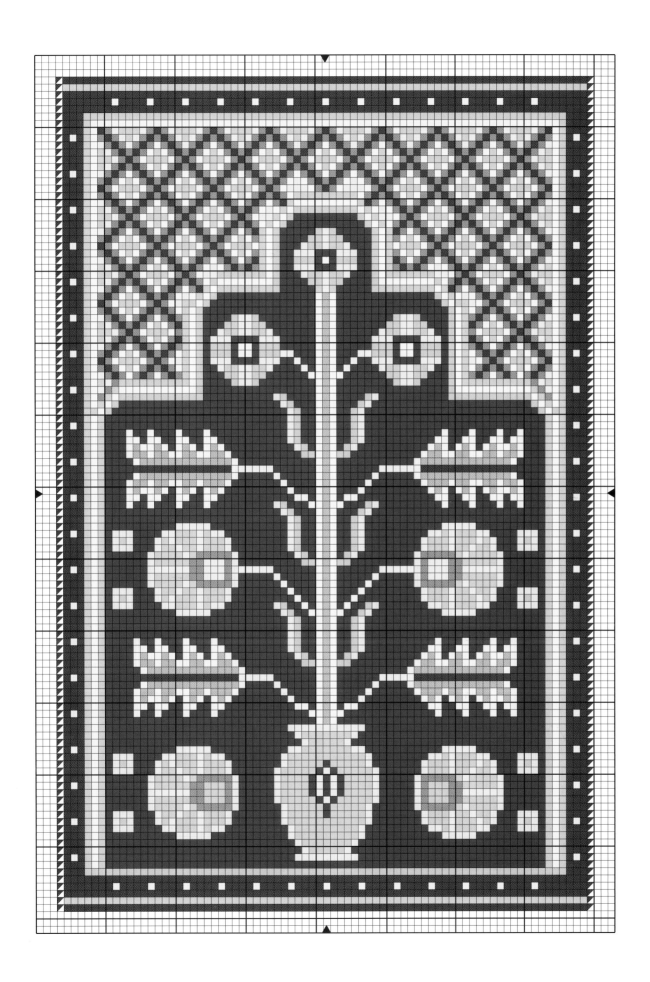

EAST TURKESTAN PRAYER RUG

Ch'i Lin Rug

For this rug I have adapted a nineteenth-century chair cover design featuring a mythical creature called a Ch'i lin. This creature corresponds to a unicorn and acts as a judge, sparing innocents, but using its horns to strike the guilty. Emperors sometimes claimed to have seen a Ch'i lin in their dreams, and thought it brought messages from heaven. I could not resist adapting this lovely border of waves and pearls and the golden animal to make this charming rug.

Threads required

	Anchor Stranded Cotton	Amount
	847	202cm (79⁹⁄₁₀in)
	1034	147.6cm (58¹⁄₁₀in)
	1036	131.7cm (51⁹⁄₁₀in)
	361	130.4cm (51³⁄₁₀in)
	877	136.1cm (53⁶⁄₁₀in)
	890	237.8cm (93⁶⁄₁₀in)
	1004	396.9cm (156³⁄₁₀in)
	306	224.5cm (88⁴⁄₁₀in)
	901	67.2cm (26⁵⁄₁₀in)
	150	4229.6cm (1665²⁄₁₀in)
	386	55.7cm (21⁹⁄₁₀in)
	150*	122.9cm (48⁴⁄₁₀in)

*Work at end using 6 strands

Design size	11.4 x 16cm (4½ x 6⁵⁄₂in)
Stitch count	99 x 139
Number of strands	3
Number of strands for fringe	6
Thread for fringe	Anchor Stranded Cotton 847

CH'I LIN RUG

Khotan Carpet

This was designed using components from a nineteenth-century carpet that looked almost like a 'sampler' of patterns, which seemed to be haphazardly placed on the field of the carpet. It had an interestingly broken swastika border, which looks quite dazzling when worked in these colours.

Design size	8.7 x 13.4cm ($3\frac{13}{32}$ x $5\frac{9}{32}$in)
Stitch count	75 x 116
Number of strands	3
Number of strands for fringe	6
Thread for fringe	Anchor Stranded Cotton 386

Threads required

	Anchor Stranded Cotton	Amount
	1014	184.3cm ($72\frac{6}{10}$in)
	150	341.7cm ($134\frac{5}{10}$in)
	386	298.8cm ($117\frac{6}{10}$in)
	5975	1071.4cm ($421\frac{8}{10}$in)
	146	827.4cm ($325\frac{8}{10}$in)
	306	80.4cm ($31\frac{7}{10}$in)
	69	938.8cm ($369\frac{6}{10}$in)
	69*	102.5cm ($40\frac{4}{10}$in)

*Work at end using 6 strands

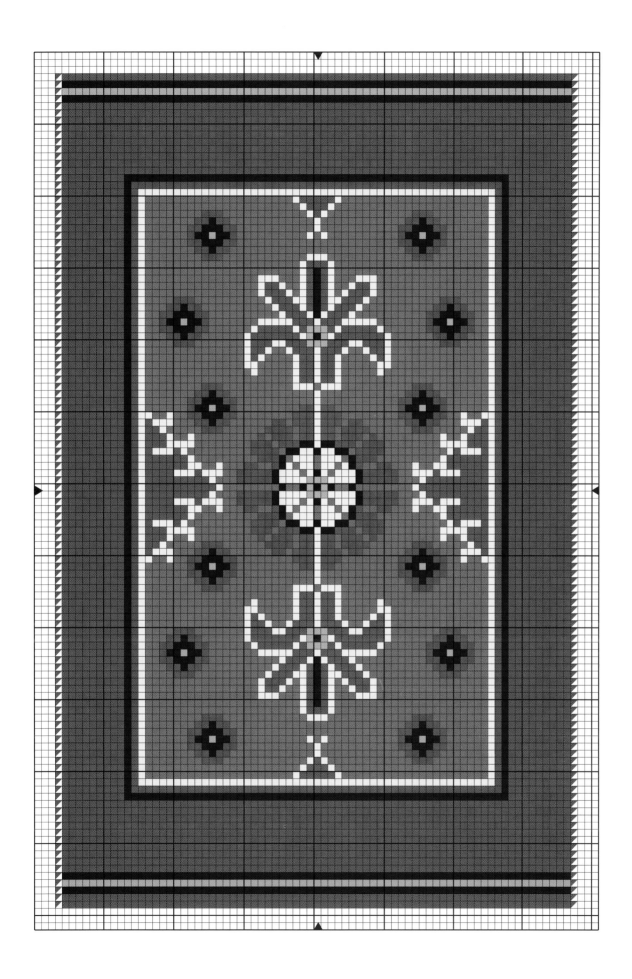

KHOTAN CARPET

Gúl Pattern Carpet

T his interesting twining destiny knot design was adapted from an eighteenth-century vertical scroll painting on silk. It was a portrait by an anonymous artist of the Emperor Qianlong who died in 1799. The carpet was painted on the floor around the wooden or leather dais. It was just possible to identify the key border at the back of the painting.

Design size	12.1 x 16.3cm (3¾ x 6¹³/₃₂in)
Stitch count	105 x 141
Number of strands	3
Number of strands for fringe	6
Thread for fringe	Anchor Stranded Cotton 1037

Threads required

	Anchor Stranded Cotton	Amount
	683	1549.7cm (610¹/₁₀in)
	215	479.1cm (188⁶/₁₀in)
	213	440.2cm (173³/₁₀in)
	1037	1294.2cm (509⁵/₁₀in)
	140	489.7cm (192⁸/₁₀in)
	779	91.1cm (35⁹/₁₀in)
	339	357.1cm (140⁶/₁₀in)
	369	1718.1cm (676⁴/₁₀in)
	683*	124.6cm (49¹/₁₀in)

*Work at end using 6 strands

Fo-dog Carpet

The Fo-dog occurs in all Chinese art forms. It is similar to the Ch'i Lin, but is less dragon-like, without the flaming tendrils coming from the knees, head and tail. Fo-dogs were supposed to be Buddha's companions and stone statues of fo-dogs guarded holy places. They were the guardians of the home.

This rug was adapted from a small carpet from Ninghsia. Ninghsia was, at one time, a key centre for quality carpet production and the name came to be attributed more generally to all rugs of good quality. The original featured a fo-dog fighting a phoenix. As well as this scene, the rug shows peonies, the symbol of wealth, and 'Shou' characters for good luck. As before, the inclusion of swastikas enhances the wishes ten thousand times over. It is this wonderful, almost three-dimensional, linked swastika design that I found most appealing and is my main reason for including this carpet.

Design size	10.7 x 17.4cm (4⁷⁄₃₂ x 6²⁷⁄₃₂in)
Stitch count	93 x 151
Number of strands	3
Number of strands for fringe	6
Thread for fringe	Anchor Stranded Cotton 368

Threads required

	Anchor Stranded Cotton	Amount
	152	1700cm (669³⁄₁₀in)
	386	1186.8cm (467²⁄₁₀in)
	132	477.8cm (188¹⁄₁₀in)
	368 x 2, 369 x 1	2517.7cm (991²⁄₁₀in)
	150	79.6cm (31³⁄₁₀in)
	369	42cm (16⁵⁄₁₀in)
	129	69.8cm (27⁵⁄₁₀in)
	152*	133.5cm (52⁶⁄₁₀in)

*Work at end using 6 strands

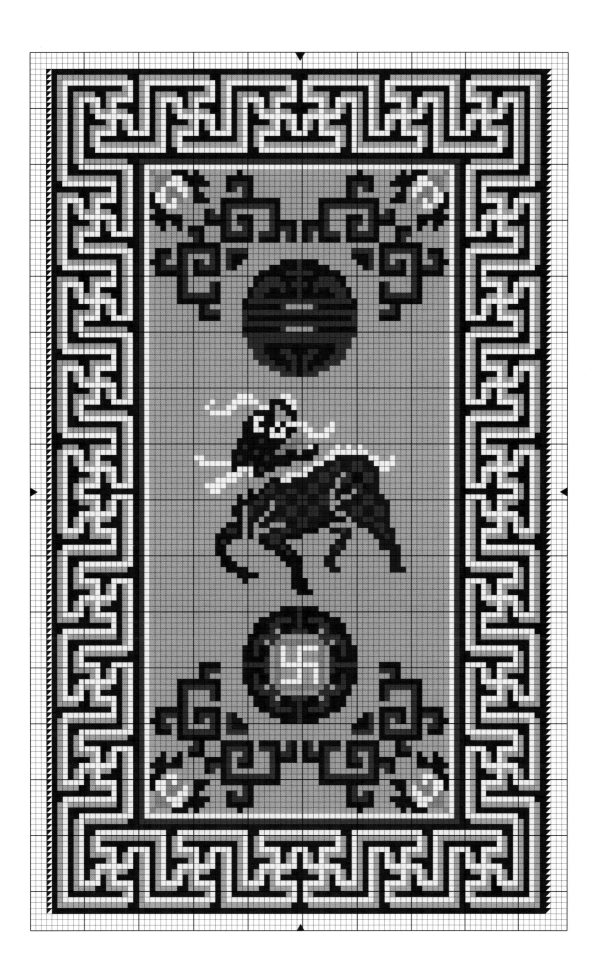

Khotan Prayer Rug

In addition to the design, it was the lovely warm colouring of this nineteenth-century prayer rug that I particularly liked. Once again, it shows the 'Tree of Life' growing from a vase, and includes the niche shape directed towards Mecca. This one came from an 'Arcaded' or 'Saph' rug which had eight mihrabs in a row. It has a 'Pearl' border.

Design size	8.2 x 14.9cm (3⁷⁄₃₂ x 5²⁷⁄₃₂in)
Stitch count	71 x 129
Number of strands	3
Number of strands for fringe	6
Thread for fringe	Anchor Stranded Cotton 5975

Threads required

	Anchor Stranded Cotton	Amount
	152	1167.8cm (459%₀in)
	5975	1394.1cm (548%₀in)
	1013	371.3cm (146²⁄₀in)
	858	189.6cm (74⁷⁄₀in)
	368	811.5cm (319%₀in)
	5975*	114cm (44%₀in)

*Work at end using 6 strands

KHOTAN PRAYER RUG

61

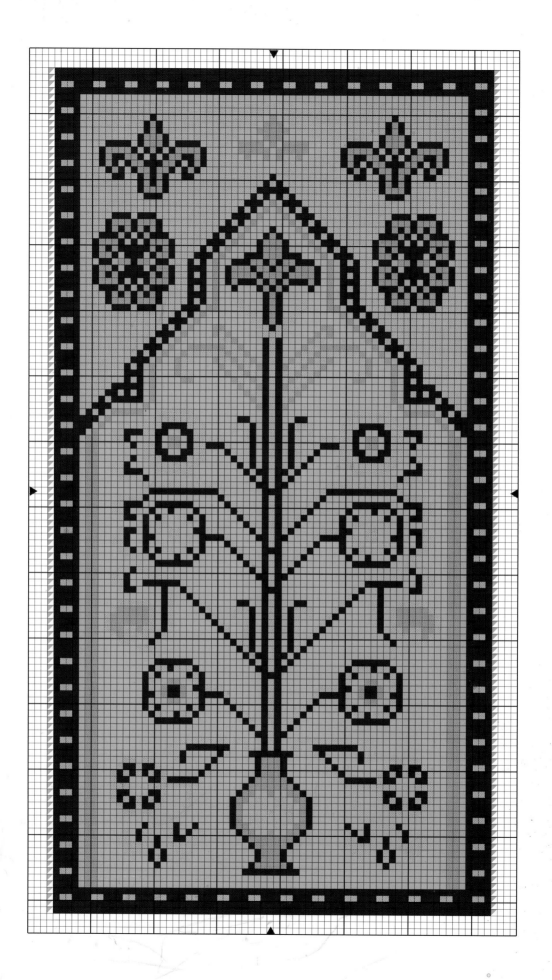

East Turkestan Brown Carpet

The colouring on the original carpet was quite different from most of the other rugs and carpets featured here, so I adapted aspects of the design to maintain a similar overall feel. Although the centre of the design represents only one tiny section of the original, I have reproduced the swastika and flower borders fairly accurately to represent a typical eighteenth-century East Turkestan carpet.

Threads required

	Anchor Stranded Cotton	Amount
	403	229.8cm (90⁵⁄₁₀in)
	886	135.7cm (53⁴⁄₁₀in)
	360	1701.7cm (690in)
	850	402.2cm (158⁴⁄₁₀in)
	311	872.1cm (343³⁄₁₀in)
	386	512.3cm (201⁷⁄₁₀in)
	369	347.4cm (136⁸⁄₁₀in)
	150	69.8cm (27⁵⁄₁₀in)
	139	80.4cm (31⁷⁄₁₀in)
	368	124.6cm (49¹⁄₁₀in)
	371	126.9cm (49⁹⁄₁₀in)
	360*	112.3cm (44²⁄₁₀in)

*Work at end using 6 strands

Design size	9.7 x 14.7cm (3¹³⁄₁₆ x 5²⁵⁄₃₂in)
Stitch count	84 x 127
Number of strands	3
Number of strands for fringe	6
Thread for fringe	Anchor Stranded Cotton 886

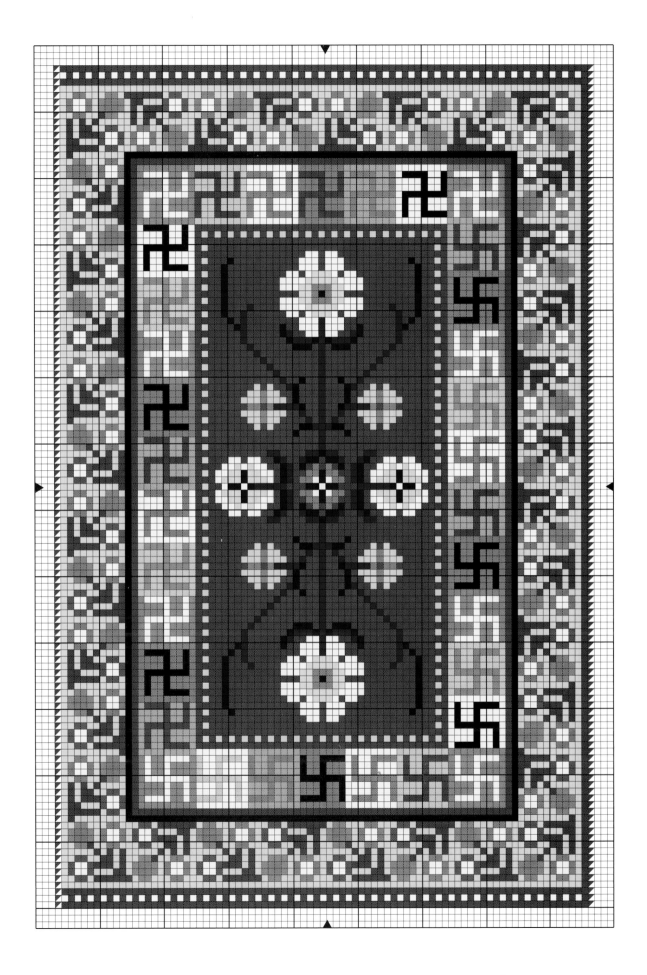

EAST TURKESTAN BROWN CARPET

65

Creature and Diamond Carpet

This design was adapted from an early nineteenth-century carpet which included a deer, crane, peonies, bats and butterflies. A stag stood for well-being and was used on official badges to designate a person's standing. The stag often had a fungus called a 'ligzhi' in its mouth which represented a wish for immortality. Manchurian cranes were also a symbol for long life and immortality and were thought to be the messengers for Shou Xing, the God of Longevity. Peonies represented wealth and were the 'King of Flowers'. The meanings associated with bats and butterflies derive from homophones. (See details in the Introduction, page 4.) A bat in Chinese is 'fu', which is also the sound for prosperity, so bats in a design were a wish for riches and prosperity. The colours in this rug are soft and harmonious and continue into the unusual diamond border, with the addition of blues.

Threads required

	Anchor Stranded Cotton	Amount
	390	2274.6cm (895⁵⁄₁₀in)
	977	554.3cm (218²⁄₁₀in)
	896	678.9cm (267³⁄₁₀in)
	895	743.9cm (292⁹⁄₁₀in)
	897	1264.1cm (497⁷⁄₁₀in)
	976	499.9cm (196⁸⁄₁₀in)
	362	585.7cm (230⁹⁄₁₀in)
	897*	128.2cm (50⁵⁄₁₀in)

*Work at end using 6 strands

Design size	12.1 x 16.7cm (4¾ x 6⁹⁄₁₆in)
Stitch count	105 x 145
Number of strands	3
Number of strands for fringe	6
Thread for fringe	Anchor Stranded Cotton 390

Suiyuan Horse Carpet

This nineteenth-century carpet is one of my favourites, because it makes me smile every time I look at it.

A number of these rugs show two horses – one at each end – fastened underneath what is often a pine tree. This arrangement symbolizes constancy, and these horses certainly do not seem to be in a hurry to gallop off! Sometimes the horse is replaced by a deer (see, for example, the saddle rug on page 2). The blue and white colouring is typical of Suiyuan rugs. In this design a saddle rug can be seen underneath the saddle. At the bottom there is a wave pattern and a variation of the mountain design.

Threads required

	Anchor Stranded Cotton	Amount
■	152	3730.6cm (1468⅞in)
■	779	403.6cm (158⅞in)
■	1062	190.5cm (75in)
■	1033	1101.5cm (433⅞in)
	1037	377.5cm (148⅞in)
	386	793.8cm (312⅝in)
	213	60.6cm (23⅞in)
■	1033 x 2, 1037 x 1	172.4cm (67⅞in)
■	779 x 2, 1062 x 1	171.5cm (67⅝in)
	213 x 1, 1037 x 2	102.1cm (40⅕in)
◣	152*	131.7cm (51⅞in)

*Work at end using 6 strands

Design size	12.4 x 17.7cm (4⅞ x 7in)
Stitch count	107 x 153
Number of strands	3
Number of strands for fringe	6
Thread for fringe	Anchor Stranded Cotton 779

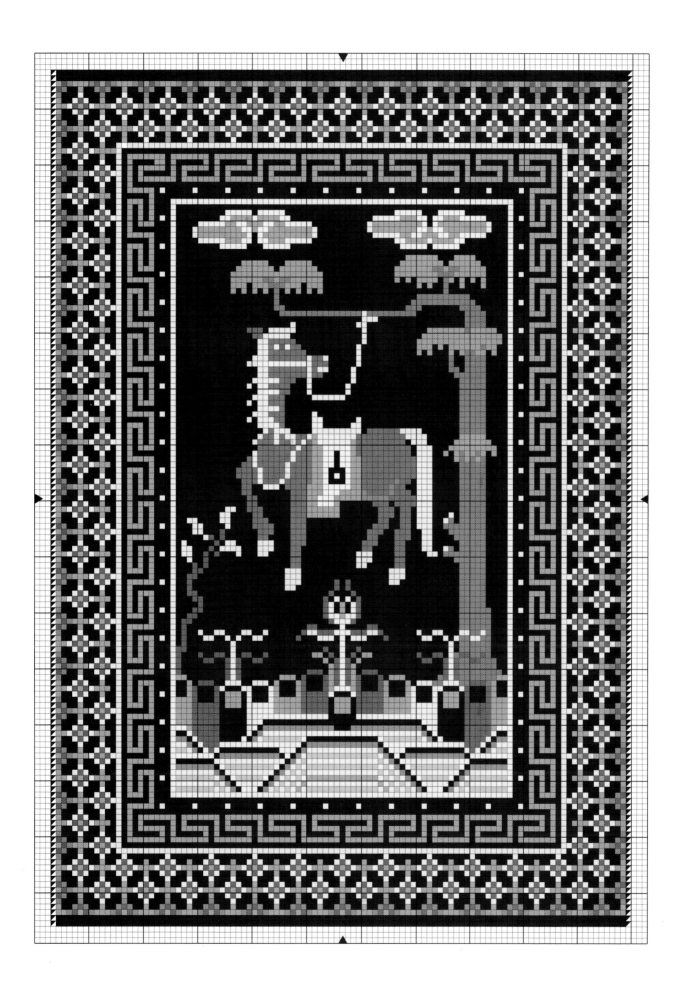

SUIYUAN HORSE CARPET

Peony Carpet

This carpet design was adapted from a large nineteenth-century carpet which was a mass of flowers and foliage in browns and dark blue. The original has a small border around the edge and I have added a complementary T-border from another nineteenth-century carpet.

Design size	9.8 x 14.5cm (3^{27}/$_{32}$ x 5^{11}/$_{16}$in)
Stitch count	85 x 126
Number of strands	3
Number of strands for fringe	6
Thread for fringe	Anchor Stranded Cotton 275

Threads required

	Anchor Stranded Cotton	Amount
	134	1564.3cm (615^9/$_{10}$in)
	891	59.7cm (23^5/$_{10}$in)
	369	1888.3cm (743^4/$_{10}$in)
	137	124.6cm (49^1/$_{10}$in)
	140	633.8cm (249^5/$_{10}$in)
	386	351.8cm (138^5/$_{10}$in)
	134*	111.4cm (43^9/$_{10}$in)

*Work at end using 6 strands

PEONY CARPET

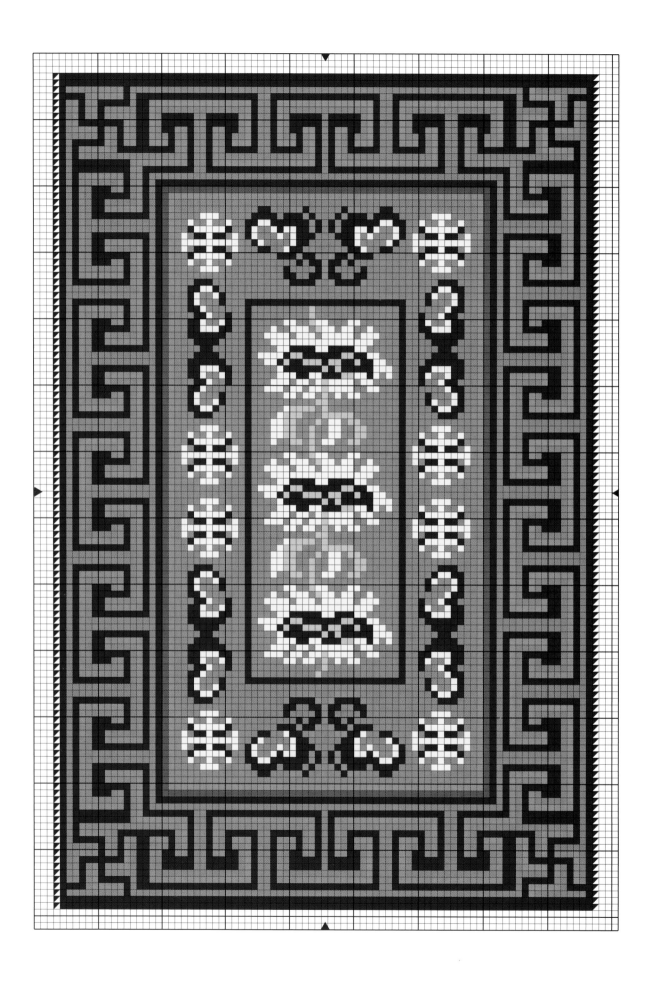

Silk Herati Carpet

This is a simplified version of an eighteenth-century silk rug. The background was woven with plaited gold metallic thread. To achieve this effect, the silk pattern was first knotted then the metallic thread woven flatly over top of it, so that the silk pattern appeared in relief. The field is based on a Herati design, which is composed of a rosette surrounded by lance-shaped leaves which, together, form a kind of diamond. The border is a simple key pattern. The original was lined with pure red silk. Being underneath, this cannot be seen, but apparently it was often the case in China that the best treasures were hidden away to be shown only to those people who appreciated them.

Threads required

	Kreinik Silk Mori	Amount
	5095	252.8cm (99⅝in)
	5055	224.5cm (88⅜in)
	7128	5.7cm (2³⁄₁₀in)
	2063	158.2cm (62³⁄₁₀in)
	2066	773.5cm (304⁵⁄₁₀in)
	7126	1422.4cm (560in)
	5057	709cm (279¹⁄₁₀in)
	5057*	99.9cm (39³⁄₁₀in)

*Work at end using 6 strands

Design size	8.4 x 13cm (3⁷⁄₁₆ x 5⅛in)
Stitch count	73 x 113
Number of strands	3
Number of strands for fringe	6
Thread for fringe	Kreinik Silk Mori 7126

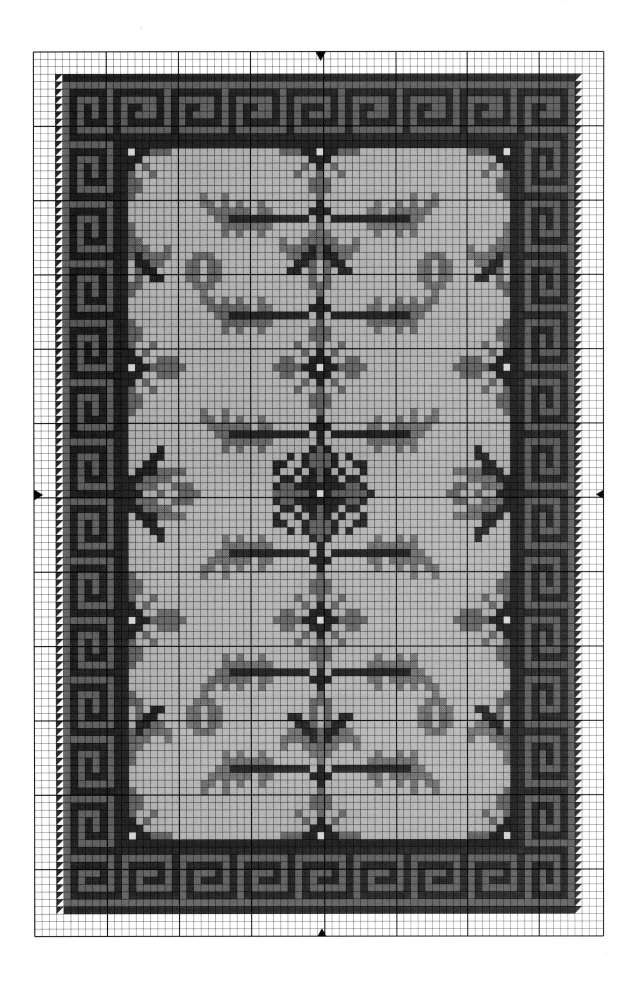

SILK HERATI CARPET

Peony Medallion Carpet

This rug design was adapted from an early nineteenth-century Kansu original. It shows a medallion with peonies, the character for wealth. The central design is framed by a 'Pearl' border. The external border is composed of linked swastikas which symbolize many blessings and good luck. The original carpet may have been made from camel's wool.

Design size	10.3 x 17.4cm (4 x 6²⁷⁄₃₂in)
Stitch count	89 x 151
Number of strands	3
Number of strands for fringe	6
Thread for fringe	Anchor Stranded Cotton 368

Threads required

	Anchor Stranded Cotton	Amount
	884	126.4cm (49⁸⁄₁₀in)
	150	2328.1cm (916⁶⁄₁₀in)
	147	443.8cm (174⁷⁄₁₀in)
	129	105.2cm (41⁴⁄₁₀in)
	368	2691cm (1059⁴⁄₁₀in)
	386	112.3cm (44²⁄₁₀in)
	150*	133.5cm (52⁶⁄₁₀in)

*Work at end using 6 strands

PEONY MEDALLION CARPET

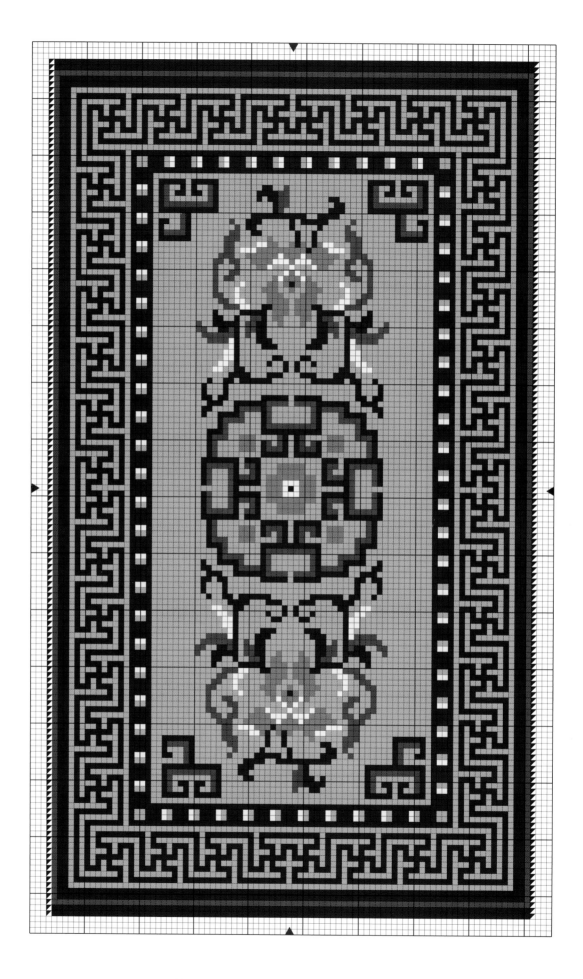

Black Velvet Rug

This seventeenth-century rug was made of velvet, which was woven and cut so that the colours changed with the direction of the light. It shows a lotus medallion, the symbol for purity. The foliage and bats in each corner signify a wish for riches and prosperity. It has a border made up of linked swastikas which means that the blessings are multiplied many times over.

Design size	12.8 x 15.1cm (5 x 6in)
Stitch count	111 x 131
Number of strands	3
Number of strands for fringe	6
Thread for fringe	Anchor Stranded Cotton 386

Threads required

	Anchor Stranded Cotton	Amount
	403	4070.5cm (1602⅝in)
	386	1564.7cm (616in)
	390	178.6cm (70⅜in)
	6	188.3cm (74¼in)
	9	8.8cm (3⅝in)
	11	93.7cm (36⅞in)
	10	206.9cm (81⅜in)
	403*	115.8cm (45⅝in)

*Work at end using 6 strands

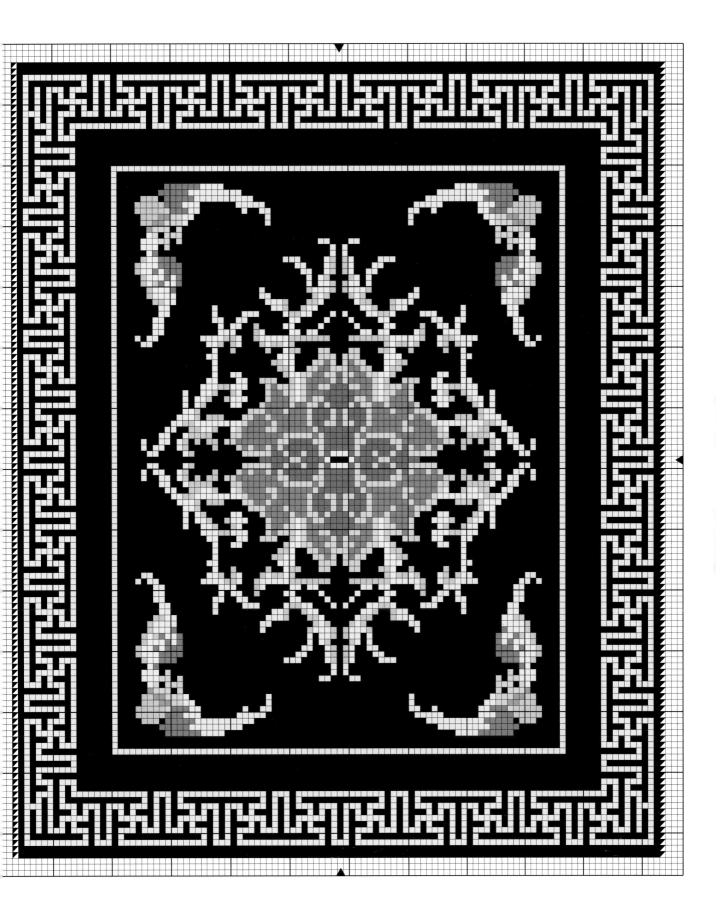

BLACK VELVET RUG

Kansu Destiny Knot Carpet

This dramatic rug has a similar central medallion to the Peony Medallion Carpet (see page 78). It is typical of the blue and white rugs from Kansu. Again, although it is called a Kansu rug, it does not necessarily mean that it was actually woven in Kansu, but more likely exported from here and taken along the Silk Route to the Mediterranean. This rug has a design utilizing creeping peonies, the symbol of wealth, and destiny knots which are shown in the brocade border. These symbolize a safe journey through life and a peaceful end under Buddha's protection. The carpet also has a dotted 'Pearl' border around the centre framed by a T-border.

Threads required

	Anchor Stranded Cotton	Amount
▬	152	2597.2cm (1022⅖in)
	386	2623.3cm (1032⅞in)
▬	149	1223.5cm (481⅞in)
▬	147	769.1cm (302⅞in)
▬	145	599.4cm (236in)
◣	152*	154.7cm (60⅞in)

*Work at end using 6 strands

Design size	11.9 x 20.2cm (4¹¹⁄₁₆ x 8¹⁵⁄₁₆in)
Stitch count	103 x 175
Number of strands	3
Number of strands for fringe	6
Thread for fringe	Anchor Stranded Cotton 275

KANSU DESTINY KNOT CARPET

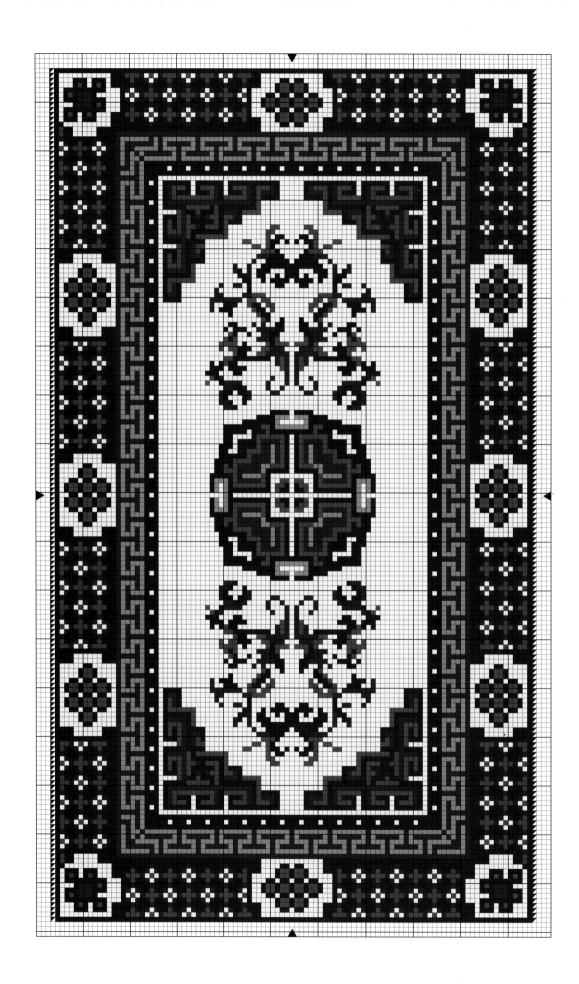

Thread
Conversion Chart

This conversion chart is for guidance only,
as exact comparisons are not always possible.

Anchor	DMC	Madeira	Kreinik	Appletons
1	blanc	2401	8000	991B
6	353	2605		621
9	352	303	3013	622
10	351	406	3015	623
11	350	213		625
20	3777	2502		504
69	3685	2609		146
121	793	906		744
123	3750	914		465
129	3325	907		462
132	797	912	5095	822
133	796	913		823
134	820	914	5097	824
137	798	911		821
139	797	912		823
140	3755	910		462
145	799	910		744
146	798	911		463
147	797	912		464
148	311	1005	5014	*
149	336	1006		*

Anchor	DMC	Madeira	Kreinik	Appletons
150	823	1007		749
152	939	1009	5016	852
176	793	906		744
213	369	1511	4073	151
214	368	2604		641
215	320	1310		642
268	937	1504		547
275	746	101	7124	882
279	734	1610		312
295	726	109	2024	471
297	973	105	2026	694
306	725	2514		474
307	783	2514		475
311	977	2301		*
323	722	307		862
326	720	309		626
333	608	206	1112	445
338	921	402		721
339	920	312		722
340	919	313		722
341	355	314		724
360	938	2005		187
361	738	2013		*
362	437	2012		*
365	434	2213		765
368	436	2011		*
369	435	2010		*
371	433	2602		905
380	838	2005	7136	187
386	746	2512	7082/7128	881
387	ecru	2314	7128	992
390	822	1908		877
403	310	2400	8050	993
683	890	1705	4067/4077	835

Anchor	DMC	Madeira	Kreinik	Appletons
779	3768	2508		323
831	3732	2109	7014	761
843	3012	1606		343
847	928	1805		875
850	926	1707		321
858	524	1512	4074/4203	341
868	758	403		351
874	834	2510	2014/7086	694
877	502	1205	4164	642
884	400	2305		863
886	3047	2207		691
887	3046	2206	7086	693
890	729	2209		*
891	676	2208		*
895	223	812		754
896	315	810		756
897	221	2606		759
901	435	2210		903
943	422	2102		760
976	3752	1002		562
1003	922	310	2063	863
1004	920	312	2066	722
1013	3778	2310		205
1014	355	2502		726
1033	932	1710		742
1034	931	1711	5055	924
1036	336	1712	5057	925
1037	3756	2504	5091	875
1062	597	1101		563
1082	842	1909	7133	182
1084	841	1912	7134	183
1088	839	2005	7135	187
4146	950	2309	3021	621
5975	356	401		721

About the Author

Carol was born in Scarborough, North Yorkshire, but has lived in the East Riding of Yorkshire for many years with her husband Alan and their two daughters.

She trained as a teacher, and still teaches part-time in her village school. She has always been interested in embroidery and design, and with a friend started a needlework business. This has now been sold, and for many years Carol has been a freelance needlework designer, working mainly for magazines and kit companies.

She spends a lot of time walking in the Derbyshire Dales, but some form of embroidery is always at hand. Carol thinks that one of the nicest things about stitching is that it is so portable and can be done almost anywhere.

Carol's previous titles for GMC Publications Ltd are *Celtic Cross Stitch Designs* and *Cross-Stitch Designs from China*.

Index

Titles of projects are in *italics*.

TITLES AVAILABLE FROM
GMC Publications
BOOKS

WOODCARVING

The Art of the Woodcarver	GMC Publications
Beginning Woodcarving	GMC Publications
Carving Architectural Detail in Wood: The Classical Tradition	
	Frederick Wilbur
Carving Birds & Beasts	GMC Publications
Carving the Human Figure: Studies in Wood and Stone	Dick Onians
Carving Nature: Wildlife Studies in Wood	Frank Fox-Wilson
Carving Realistic Birds	David Tippey
Decorative Woodcarving	Jeremy Williams
Elements of Woodcarving	Chris Pye
Essential Woodcarving Techniques	Dick Onians
Lettercarving in Wood: A Practical Course	Chris Pye
Making & Using Working Drawings for Realistic Model Animals	
	Basil F. Fordham
Power Tools for Woodcarving	David Tippey
Relief Carving in Wood: A Practical Introduction	Chris Pye
Understanding Woodcarving	GMC Publications
Understanding Woodcarving in the Round	GMC Publications
Useful Techniques for Woodcarvers	GMC Publications
Wildfowl Carving – Volume 1	Jim Pearce
Wildfowl Carving – Volume 2	Jim Pearce
Woodcarving: A Complete Course	Ron Butterfield
Woodcarving: A Foundation Course	Zoë Gertner
Woodcarving for Beginners	GMC Publications
Woodcarving Tools & Equipment Test Reports	GMC Publications
Woodcarving Tools, Materials & Equipment	Chris Pye

WOODTURNING

Adventures in Woodturning	David Springett
Bert Marsh: Woodturner	Bert Marsh
Bowl Turning Techniques Masterclass	Tony Boase
Colouring Techniques for Woodturners	Jan Sanders
Contemporary Turned Wood: New Perspectives in a Rich Tradition	
	Ray Leier, Jan Peters & Kevin Wallace
The Craftsman Woodturner	Peter Child
Decorating Turned Wood: The Maker's Eye	Liz & Michael O'Donnell
Decorative Techniques for Woodturners	Hilary Bowen
Fun at the Lathe	R.C. Bell
Illustrated Woodturning Techniques	John Hunnex

Intermediate Woodturning Projects	GMC Publications
Keith Rowley's Woodturning Projects	Keith Rowley
Making Screw Threads in Wood	Fred Holder
Turned Boxes: 50 Designs	Chris Stott
Turning Green Wood	Michael O'Donnell
Turning Miniatures in Wood	John Sainsbury
Turning Pens and Pencils	Kip Christensen & Rex Burningham
Understanding Woodturning	Ann & Bob Phillips
Useful Techniques for Woodturners	GMC Publications
Useful Woodturning Projects	GMC Publications
Woodturning: Bowls, Platters, Hollow Forms, Vases, Vessels, Bottles, Flasks, Tankards, Plates	GMC Publications
Woodturning: A Foundation Course (New Edition)	Keith Rowley
Woodturning: A Fresh Approach	Robert Chapman
Woodturning: An Individual Approach	Dave Regester
Woodturning: A Source Book of Shapes	John Hunnex
Woodturning Jewellery	Hilary Bowen
Woodturning Masterclass	Tony Boase
Woodturning Techniques	GMC Publications
Woodturning Tools & Equipment Test Reports	GMC Publications
Woodturning Wizardry	David Springett

WOODWORKING

Advanced Scrollsaw Projects	GMC Publications
Beginning Picture Marquetry	Lawrence Threadgold
Bird Boxes and Feeders for the Garden	Dave Mackenzie
Complete Woodfinishing	Ian Hosker
David Charlesworth's Furniture-Making Techniques	David Charlesworth
David Charlesworth's Furniture-Making Techniques – Volume 2	
	David Charlesworth
The Encyclopedia of Joint Making	Terrie Noll
Furniture-Making Projects for the Wood Craftsman	GMC Publications
Furniture-Making Techniques for the Wood Craftsman	
	GMC Publications
Furniture Projects	Rod Wales
Furniture Restoration (Practical Crafts)	Kevin Jan Bonner
Furniture Restoration: A Professional at Work	John Lloyd
Furniture Restoration and Repair for Beginners	Kevin Jan Bonner
Furniture Restoration Workshop	Kevin Jan Bonner
Green Woodwork	Mike Abbott
The History of Furniture	Michael Huntley

Intarsia: 30 Patterns for the Scrollsaw — John Everett
Kevin Ley's Furniture Projects — Kevin Ley
Making & Modifying Woodworking Tools — Jim Kingshott
Making Chairs and Tables — GMC Publications
Making Chairs and Tables – Volume 2 — GMC Publications
Making Classic English Furniture — Paul Richardson
Making Heirloom Boxes — Peter Lloyd
Making Little Boxes from Wood — John Bennett
Making Screw Threads in Wood — Fred Holder
Making Shaker Furniture — Barry Jackson
Making Woodwork Aids and Devices — Robert Wearing
Mastering the Router — Ron Fox
Minidrill: Fifteen Projects — John Everett
Pine Furniture Projects for the Home — Dave Mackenzie
Practical Scrollsaw Patterns — John Everett
Router Magic: Jigs, Fixtures and Tricks to
 Unleash your Router's Full Potential — Bill Hylton
Router Tips & Techniques — Robert Wearing
Routing: A Workshop Handbook — Anthony Bailey
Routing for Beginners — Anthony Bailey
The Scrollsaw: Twenty Projects — John Everett
Sharpening: The Complete Guide — Jim Kingshott
Sharpening Pocket Reference Book — Jim Kingshott
Simple Scrollsaw Projects — GMC Publications
Space-Saving Furniture Projects — Dave Mackenzie
Stickmaking: A Complete Course — Andrew Jones & Clive George
Stickmaking Handbook — Andrew Jones & Clive George
Storage Projects for the Router — GMC Publications
Test Reports: The Router and Furniture & Cabinetmaking — GMC Publications
Veneering: A Complete Course — Ian Hosker
Veneering Handbook — Ian Hosker
Woodfinishing Handbook (Practical Crafts) — Ian Hosker
Woodworking with the Router: Professional
 Router Techniques any Woodworker can Use — Bill Hylton & Fred Matlack
The Workshop — Jim Kingshott

UPHOLSTERY
The Upholsterer's Pocket Reference Book — David James
Upholstery: A Complete Course (Revised Edition) — David James
Upholstery Restoration — David James
Upholstery Techniques & Projects — David James
Upholstery Tips and Hints — David James

TOYMAKING
Restoring Rocking Horses — Clive Green & Anthony Dew
Scrollsaw Toy Projects — Ivor Carlyle
Scrollsaw Toys for All Ages — Ivor Carlyle

DOLLS' HOUSES AND MINIATURES
1/12 Scale Character Figures for the Dolls' House — James Carrington
Architecture for Dolls' Houses — Joyce Percival
The Authentic Georgian Dolls' House — Brian Long
A Beginners' Guide to the Dolls' House Hobby — Jean Nisbett
Celtic, Medieval and Tudor Wall Hangings in 1/12 Scale Needlepoint — Sandra Whitehead
The Complete Dolls' House Book — Jean Nisbett
The Dolls' House 1/24 Scale: A Complete Introduction — Jean Nisbett
Dolls' House Accessories, Fixtures and Fittings — Andrea Barham
Dolls' House Bathrooms: Lots of Little Loos — Patricia King
Dolls' House Fireplaces and Stoves — Patricia King
Dolls' House Makeovers — Jean Nisbett
Dolls' House Window Treatments — Eve Harwood
Easy to Make Dolls' House Accessories — Andrea Barham
Heraldic Miniature Knights — Peter Greenhill
How to Make Your Dolls' House Special: Fresh Ideas for Decorating — Beryl Armstrong
Make Your Own Dolls' House Furniture — Maurice Harper
Making Dolls' House Furniture — Patricia King
Making Georgian Dolls' Houses — Derek Rowbottom
Making Miniature Food and Market Stalls — Angie Scarr
Making Miniature Gardens — Freida Gray
Making Miniature Oriental Rugs & Carpets — Meik & Ian McNaughton
Making Period Dolls' House Accessories — Andrea Barham
Making Tudor Dolls' Houses — Derek Rowbottom
Making Victorian Dolls' House Furniture — Patricia King
Miniature Bobbin Lace — Roz Snowden
Miniature Embroidery for the Georgian Dolls' House — Pamela Warner
Miniature Embroidery for the Tudor and Stuart Dolls' House — Pamela Warner
Miniature Embroidery for the Victorian Dolls' House — Pamela Warner
Miniature Needlepoint Carpets — Janet Granger
More Miniature Oriental Rugs & Carpets — Meik & Ian McNaughton
Needlepoint 1/12 Scale: Design Collections for the Dolls' House — Felicity Price
New Ideas for Miniature Bobbin Lace — Roz Snowden
The Secrets of the Dolls' House Makers — Jean Nisbett

CRAFTS
American Patchwork Designs in Needlepoint — Melanie Tacon
A Beginners' Guide to Rubber Stamping — Brenda Hunt
Beginning Picture Marquetry — Lawrence Threadgold
Blackwork: A New Approach — Brenda Day
Celtic Cross Stitch Designs — Carol Phillipson
Celtic Knotwork Designs — Sheila Sturrock
Celtic Knotwork Handbook — Sheila Sturrock
Celtic Spirals and Other Designs — Sheila Sturrock
Collage from Seeds, Leaves and Flowers — Joan Carver

GARDENING

PHOTOGRAPHY

VIDEOS

Drop-in and Pinstuffed Seats	*David James*	Twists and Advanced Turning	*Dennis White*
Stuffover Upholstery	*David James*	Sharpening the Professional Way	*Jim Kingshott*
Elliptical Turning	*David Springett*	Sharpening Turning & Carving Tools	*Jim Kingshott*
Woodturning Wizardry	*David Springett*	Bowl Turning	*John Jordan*
Turning Between Centres: The Basics	*Dennis White*	Hollow Turning	*John Jordan*
Turning Bowls	*Dennis White*	Woodturning: A Foundation Course	*Keith Rowley*
Boxes, Goblets and Screw Threads	*Dennis White*	Carving a Figure: The Female Form	*Ray Gonzalez*
Novelties and Projects	*Dennis White*	The Router: A Beginner's Guide	*Alan Goodsell*
Classic Profiles	*Dennis White*	The Scroll Saw: A Beginner's Guide	*John Burke*

MAGAZINES

WOODTURNING ◆ WOODCARVING ◆ FURNITURE & CABINETMAKING
THE ROUTER ◆ WOODWORKING
THE DOLLS' HOUSE MAGAZINE
OUTDOOR PHOTOGRAPHY ◆ BLACK & WHITE PHOTOGRAPHY
BUSINESSMATTERS

The above represents a full list of all titles currently published or scheduled to be published.
All are available direct from the Publishers or through bookshops, newsagents and specialist retailers.
To place an order, or to obtain a complete catalogue, contact:

**GMC Publications,
Castle Place, 166 High Street, Lewes, East Sussex BN7 1XU, United Kingdom
Tel: 01273 488005 Fax: 01273 478606
E-mail: pubs@thegmcgroup.com**

Orders by credit card are accepted

Pao Tao

Peking

Tientsin

Yarkand

YELLOW RIVER

YELLOW
SEA

tan

C H I N A

TIBET

NINGSIA

YANGTSE RIVER

EAST
CHINA
SEA

INDIA

RIVER GANGES

MEKONG RIVER

SOUTH CHINA SEA

N

BAY OF
BENGAL